D0853795

Focus on
Geometry

AN INTEGRATED APPROACH

ALAN R. HOFFER

ROBERTA KOSS

Jerry D. Beckmann • Phillip E. Duren • Julia L. Hernandez

Beth M. Schlesinger • Catherine Wiehe

PROGRAM CONCEPTUALIZERS

Barbara Alcala

Randall I. Charles

John A. Dossey

Betty M. Foxx

Alan R. Hoffer

Roberta Koss

Sid Rachlin

Freddie L. Renfro

Cathy L. Seeley

Charles B. Vonder Embse

Scott Foresman
Addison Wesley

Editorial Offices: Menlo Park, California • Glenview, Illinois
Sales Offices: Reading, Massachusetts • Atlanta, Georgia •
Glenview, Illinois • Carrollton, Texas • Menlo Park, California

1-800-552-2259
http://www.sf.aw.com

Cover images

Front

Armillary (predecessor to the astrolabe) from the Vatican/ Black, Mary
(Navajo/Paiute). Wedding Basket. 1989. Museum of Northern Arizona.

Back

Top left: Photo of financial district, Toronto, Ontario/ Klee, Paul. Castle and Sun. 1928.
Private Collection, London, Great Britain. *Top right:* Kabotie, Michael (Hopi). Kachina
Song Poetry. 1985. Acrylic on canvas/ Photo of circuit board. *Bottom left:* Armillary
(predecessor to the astrolabe) from the Vatican/ Black, Mary (Navajo/Paiute).
Wedding Basket. 1989. Museum of Northern Arizona. *Bottom right:* Italian ceramic
tile/ Fractal from the Mandelbrot Set.

Many of the designations used by manufacturers and sellers to distinguish their products are
claimed as trademarks. When those designations appear in this book and Addison-Wesley
was aware of a trademark claim, the designations have been printed in initial capital letters
(e.g., Coca-Cola).

The Major League Baseball Club insignias depicted on page 750 are reproduced with the
permission of Major League Baseball Properties and are the exclusive property of the respective
Major League Clubs and may not be reproduced without their written consent.

Copyright © 1998 by Addison Wesley Longman

All rights reserved. No part of this publication may be reproduced, stored in a retrieval
system, or transmitted, in any form or by any means, electronic, mechanical, photocopying,
recording or otherwise, without the prior written consent of the publisher.

Printed in the United States of America.

ISBN 0-201-86970-5

1 2 3 4 5 6 7 8 9 10 – VH – 99 98 97

PROGRAM CONCEPTUALIZERS

Barbara Alcala
Whittier High School
Whittier, California

Randall I. Charles
San Jose State University
San Jose, California

John A. Dossey
Illinois State University
Normal, Illinois

Betty M. Foxx
Collins High School
Chicago, Illinois

Alan R. Hoffer
University of California
Irvine, California

Roberta Koss
Redwood High School
Larkspur, California

Sid Rachlin
East Carolina University
Greenville, North Carolina

Freddie L. Renfro
Goose Creek Independent
School District
Baytown, Texas

Cathy L. Seeley
(Formerly) Texas
Education Agency
Austin, Texas

Charles B. Vonder Embse
Central Michigan University
Mt. Pleasant, Michigan

FOCUS ON GEOMETRY AUTHORS

Alan R. Hoffer
Lead author
University of California
Irvine, California

Roberta Koss
Associate lead author
Redwood High School
Larkspur, California

Jerry D. Beckmann
East High School
Lincoln, Nebraska

Phillip E. Duren
California State University
Hayward, California

Julia L. Hernandez
Rosemead High School
Rosemead, California

Beth M. Schlesinger
San Diego High School
San Diego, California

Catherine Wiehe
San Jose High Academy
San Jose, California

OTHER SERIES AUTHORS

Barbara Alcala
Whittier High School
Whittier, California

Penelope P. Booth
Baltimore County Public Schools
Towson, Maryland

Randall I. Charles
San Jose State University
San Jose, California

James R. Choike
Oklahoma State University
Stillwater, Oklahoma

David S. Daniels
Longmeadow High School
Longmeadow, Massachusetts

John A. Dossey
Illinois State University
Normal, Illinois

Trudi Hammel Garland
The Head-Royce School
Oakland, California

Pamela Patton Giles
Jordan School District
Sandy, Utah

Virginia Gray
South Medford High School
Medford, Oregon

Howard C. Johnson
Syracuse University
Syracuse, New York

Stephen E. Moresh
City College of New York
(Formerly) Seward Park
High School
New York, New York

J. Irene Murphy
North Slope Borough
School District
Barrow, Alaska

Andy Reeves
Florida Department of Education
Tallahassee, Florida

Kathy A. Ross
(Formerly) Jefferson Parish
Public School System
Harvey, Louisiana

Cathy L. Seeley
(Formerly) Texas
Education Agency
Austin, Texas

Alba González Thompson
(In memoriam)

Charles B. Vonder Embse
Central Michigan University
Mt. Pleasant, Michigan

Sheryl M. Yamada
Beverly Hills High School
Beverly Hills, California

CONSULTANTS AND REVIEWERS

CONTENT REVIEWERS

Bridget Arvold
University of Georgia
Athens, Georgia

Paul G. Dillenberger
Franklin Middle School
Minneapolis, Minnesota

Catherine Y. Figuracion
San Pedro High School
San Pedro, California

Donald Hastings
Stratford Public Schools
Stratford, Connecticut

Melanie Hildreth
Walnut High School
Walnut, California

Jim Velo
West High School
Columbus, Ohio

Joanne Wainscott
Mission Bay High School
San Diego, California

Denise Walston
Maury High School
Norfolk, Virginia

Dr. Art W. Wilson
Abraham Lincoln High School
Denver, Colorado

MULTICULTURAL REVIEWERS

LaVerne Bitsie
Oklahoma State University
Stillwater, Oklahoma

Claudette Bradley
University of Alaska
Fairbanks, Alaska

Yolanda De La Cruz
Arizona State University West
Phoenix, Arizona

Genevieve Lau
Skyline College
San Bruno, California

William Tate
University of Wisconsin
Madison, Wisconsin

INDUSTRY CONSULTANTS

Joseph M. Cahalen
Xerox Corporation
Stamford, Connecticut

Clare DeYonker
AMATECH
Bingham Farms, Michigan

Harry Garland
Cannon Research Center
America, Inc.
Palo Alto, California

Timothy M. Schwalm, Sr.
Eastman Kodak Company
Rochester, New York

Diane Sotos
Maxim Integrated Products
Sunnyvale, California

Earl R. Westerlund
Eastman Kodak Company
Rochester, New York

Charles Young
General Electric Research and
Development Center
Schenectady, New York

John Zils
Skidmore, Owings & Merrill
Chicago, Illinois

Table of Contents

Getting Started: What Do YOU Think?   i
    Part A   Working Together   ii
    Part B   Solving Problems   iv
    Part C   Making Connections   vi

CHAPTER 1   Visual Thinking and Mathematical Models   2

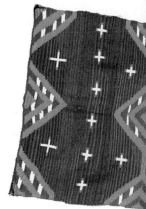

    1-1   **Using Familiar Models**   5
    Part A   Geometric Models   6
    Part B   Algebraic Models   11
    Part C   Making Connections   16

    1-2   **Reasoning and Logic**   19
    Part A   Inductive Reasoning   20
    Part B   The Language of Logic   25
    Part C   Deductive Reasoning   30
    Part D   Making Connections   36

    1-3   **Measuring Figures**   39
    Part A   Measuring Segments   40
    Part B   Measuring Angles   45
    Part C   Congruence   52
    Part D   Making Connections   58

    1-4   **Symmetry and Reflections**   61
    Part A   Symmetry   62
    Part B   Reflections   67
    Part C   Properties of Reflections   73
    Part D   Making Connections   77

CHAPTER 1   Review *(Key Terms, Concepts and Applications,*
Concepts and Connections, Self-Evaluation)   80

CHAPTER 1   Assessment *(Test, Performance Task)*   82

CHAPTER 2   The Foundations of Geometry   84

    2-1   **The Need for Precise Language**   87
    Part A   Conditional Statements   88
    Part B   Related Conditional Statements   94
    Part C   The Rules of Logic   99
    Part D   Making Connections   104

	2-2	**Stating Our Assumptions**	107
	Part A	Undefined Terms and Definitions	108
	Part B	Postulates	114
	Part C	Working in a Deductive System	119
	Part D	Making Connections	126

	2-3	**Drawing Techniques and Parallel Lines**	129
	Part A	Perspective Drawing	130
	Part B	Orthographic and Isometric Drawing	135
	Part C	Parallel Lines and Planes	141
	Part D	Making Connections	146

CHAPTER 2 **Review** *(Key Terms, Concepts and Applications, Concepts and Connections, Self-Evaluation)* 149

CHAPTER 2 **Assessment** *(Test, Performance Task)* 150

CHAPTER 3 **Angles and Parallel Lines** 152

	3-1	**Angles and Navigation**	155
	Part A	More About Rays and Angles	156
	Part B	Bearings	161
	Part C	Vectors	165
	Part D	Translations	171
	Part E	Making Connections	176

	3-2	**Rotations**	179
	Part A	Rotational Symmetry	180
	Part B	Rotations	185
	Part C	Making Connections	189

	3-3	**Precise Thinking with Angles**	191
	Part A	Postulates About Angles	192
	Part B	Assumptions and Figures	197
	Part C	Angle Pairs	201
	Part D	Vertical Angles and Angle Bisectors	207
	Part E	Making Connections	212

	3-4	**Parallel Lines and Transversals**	215
	Part A	Transversals and Angles	216
	Part B	Parallel Lines, Transversals, and Angles	221
	Part C	Proving Lines Parallel	226
	Part D	Making Connections	231

CHAPTER 3 **Review** *(Key Terms, Concepts and Applications, Concepts and Connections, Self-Evaluation)* 233

CHAPTER 3 **Assessment** *(Test, Performance Task)* 235

CHAPTER 4   Triangles   **238**

4-1   **Tessellations and Triangles**   241
Part A   Angles Inside the Triangle   242
Part B   Angles Outside the Triangle   247
Part C   Making Connections   252

4-2   **Deductive Proof with Triangles**   255
Part A   Correspondence and Congruence   256
Part B   Congruent Triangles   260
Part C   Organizing a Proof   266
Part D   Corresponding Parts   274
Part E   Making Connections   281

4-3   **Properties of Special Triangles**   285
Part A   Isosceles Triangles   286
Part B   Right Triangles   292
Part C   Perpendiculars, Bisectors, and Locus   299
Part D   Lines Associated with Triangles   304
Part E   Making Connections   310

CHAPTER 4   Review (*Key Terms, Concepts and Applications,
Concepts and Connections, Self-Evaluation*)   **314**

CHAPTER 4   Assessment (*Test, Performance Task*)   **316**

CHAPTER 5   Area   **318**

5-1   **Understanding and Applying Area**   321
Part A   Area and Perimeter   322
Part B   Polynomials and Area   327
Part C   The Quadratic Formula and Area   332
Part D   Area and Probability   337
Part E   Making Connections   342

5-2   **Derivations of Area Formulas**   345
Part A   Assumptions About Area   346
Part B   Planning a Proof   352
Part C   The Area Under a Curve   357
Part D   Making Connections   362

5-3	**The Pythagorean Theorem**	365
Part A	The Pythagorean Theorem	366
Part B	Special Right Triangles	370
Part C	The Distance Formula Revisited	376
Part D	The Converse of the Pythagorean Theorem	380
Part E	Making Connections	385

CHAPTER 5   **Review** *(Key Terms, Concepts and Applications, Concepts and Connections, Self-Evaluation)*   388

CHAPTER 5   **Assessment** *(Test, Performance Task)*   390

CHAPTER 6   **Polygons and Polyhedrons**   392

6-1	**Polygons and Polyhedrons**	395
Part A	Exploring Quadrilaterals	396
Part B	Exploring Polygons	402
Part C	Exploring Polyhedrons	409
Part D	Making Connections	414

6-2	**Deductive Proof with Quadrilaterals**	417
Part A	Proofs with Parallelograms	418
Part B	Proving Quadrilaterals Are Parallelograms	423
Part C	Proofs with Special Parallelograms	427
Part D	Quadrilaterals and Coordinate Proof	433
Part E	Making Connections	438

6-3	**Regular Polygons and Polyhedrons**	441
Part A	Regular Polygons	442
Part B	Regular Polyhedrons	448
Part C	Making Connections	452

CHAPTER 6   **Review** *(Key Terms, Concepts and Applications, Concepts and Connections, Self-Evaluation)*   455

CHAPTER 6   **Assessment** *(Test, Performance Task)*   456

CHAPTER 7   **Similarity**   **458**

7-1   **Similar Figures**   **461**
Part A   Changing the Size of Figures   **462**
Part B   Similar Polygons   **468**
Part C   Areas and Perimeters of Similar Polygons   **473**
Part D   Golden Rectangles   **478**
Part E   Making Connections   **482**

7-2   **Properties of Similar Figures**   **485**
Part A   Similar Triangles   **486**
Part B   SAS Similarity   **491**
Part C   Dilations   **496**
Part D   Triangle Midsegments   **501**
Part E   Making Connections   **507**

7-3   **Trigonometry**   **511**
Part A   Trigonometric Ratios   **512**
Part B   Angles of Elevation and Depression   **518**
Part C   Vectors and Trigonometry   **523**
Part D   Making Connections   **528**

CHAPTER 7   **Review** *(Key Terms, Concepts and Applications, Concepts and Connections, Self-Evaluation)*   **531**

CHAPTER 7   **Assessment** *(Test, Performance Task)*   **534**

CHAPTER 8   **Circles and Spheres**   **536**

8-1   **Circles, Circumference, and Area**   **539**
Part A   Inscribed and Circumscribed Figures   **540**
Part B   Circles and Tangent Lines   **544**
Part C   The Circumference of a Circle   **550**
Part D   The Area of a Circle   **555**
Part E   Making Connections   **560**

8-2   **Angles, Arcs, and Chords**   563

Part A   Arcs and Central Angles   564

Part B   Arc Length and Sectors   570

Part C   Radius-Chord Conjectures   574

Part D   Making Connections   580

8-3   **The Inscribed Angle Theorem**   583

Part A   Inscribed Angles   584

Part B   Angles Formed by Secants and Tangents   588

Part C   Making Connections   594

CHAPTER 8   **Review** *(Key Terms, Concepts and Applications, Concepts and Connections, Self-Evaluation)*   597

CHAPTER 8   **Assessment** *(Test, Performance Task)*   599

CHAPTER 9   **Surface Area and Volume**   600

9-1   **Surface Area**   603

Part A   Surface Area of Prisms   604

Part B   Surface Area of Pyramids   610

Part C   Surface Area of Cylinders and Cones   614

Part D   Making Connections   620

9-2   **Volume**   623

Part A   Volume of Prisms   624

Part B   Volume of Pyramids   630

Part C   Volume of Cylinders and Cones   635

Part D   Surface Area and Volume of Spheres   639

Part E   Making Connections   644

9-3   **Similar Solids**   647

Part A   Surface Area of Similar Solids   648

Part B   Volume of Similar Solids   653

Part C   Making Connections   657

CHAPTER 9   **Review** *(Key Terms, Concepts and Applications, Concepts and Connections, Self-Evaluation)*   661

CHAPTER 9   **Assessment** *(Test, Performance Task)*   663

CHAPTER 10 **Transformations and Patterns** 664

10-1 **Putting Transformations Together** 667
Part A   Isometries 668
Part B   Compositions of Transformations 673
Part C   Transformations of Algebraic Functions 679
Part D   Making Connections 683

10-2 **Classifying Patterns** 687
Part A   Frieze Patterns 688
Part B   Wallpaper Patterns 694
Part C   Making Connections 700

CHAPTER 10 **Review** *(Key Terms, Concepts and Applications,*
Concepts and Connections, Self-Evaluation) 703

CHAPTER 10 **Assessment** *(Test, Performance Task)* 705

CHAPTER 11 **Geometric Inequalities and Optimization** 706

11-1 **Indirect Reasoning and Inequalities** 709
Part A   Indirect Reasoning 710
Part B   Inequalities in a Triangle 714
Part C   The Triangle Inequality Theorem 720
Part D   Making Connections 724

11-2 **Optimization** 727
Part A   Optimizing Areas and Perimeters 728
Part B   Optimizing Volumes and Surface Areas 734
Part C   Making Connections 740

CHAPTER 11 **Review** *(Key Terms, Concepts and Applications,*
Concepts and Connections, Self-Evaluation) 743

CHAPTER 11 **Assessment** *(Test, Performance Task)* 744

CHAPTER 12 **Astronomy and Geometric Models** **746**

    12-1 **Using Geometry to Model the Earth** **749**
    Part A Fractals **750**
    Part B Longitude and Latitude **756**
    Part C Measurement in Astronomy **762**
    Part D Making Connections **768**

    12-2 **Euclidean and Non-Euclidean Geometries** **771**
    Part A Euclidean Geometry **772**
    Part B Non-Euclidean Geometry **777**
    Part C Making Connections **782**

CHAPTER 12 **Review** *(Key Terms, Concepts and Applications,*
Concepts and Connections, Self-Evaluation) **786**

CHAPTER 12 **Assessment** *(Test, Performance Task)* **788**

REFERENCE CENTER

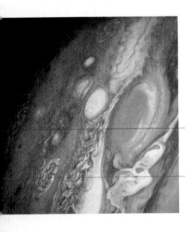

  Additional Lessons
    Proof Skills and Strategies **789**
    Graphing Linear Equations **796**
    Three-Dimensional Coordinate System **798**
    Overlapping Triangles **800**
    Compound Loci **803**
    Geometric Means and Right Triangles **805**
    Segments of Chords, Tangents, and Secants **808**
    Hinge Theorem **811**

  Spiral Review **813**
  Symbols **837**
  Formulas **838**
  Postulates and Theorems **839**
  Glossary **846**
  Selected Answers **856**
  Credits **881**
  Index **883**

Getting Started

What Do YOU Think

In the twenty-first century, computers will do a lot of the work that people used to do. Even in today's workplace, there is little need for someone to add up daily invoices or compute sales tax. Engineers and scientists already use computer programs to do calculations and solve equations. By the twenty-first century, a whole new set of skills will be needed by almost everyone in the work force.

Some important skills for the twenty-first century will be the ability to think creatively about mathematics and to reason logically. It will also be important to work as a team member and to be able to explain your thinking. Although it will still be necessary to be able to do computations, it will become increasingly necessary to analyze problems and determine the most appropriate way to solve them. After all, what good is it to solve an equation if it is the wrong equation?

This course will help you to develop many of the skills you will need for the future. On the way, you will see the value of creative thinking. The students shown here will be sharing their ideas throughout this book. But the key question will always be "What do YOU think?"

1. Why do you need to take this math class?
2. In your last math class, what was the most interesting or useful thing you learned?
3. What are some job skills that you have (or can learn) that will make it difficult to replace you with a computer?

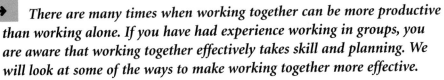

PART A Working Together

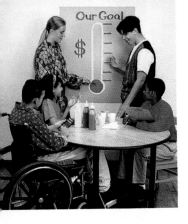

← C O N N E C T → *There are many times when working together can be more productive than working alone. If you have had experience working in groups, you are aware that working together effectively takes skill and planning. We will look at some of the ways to make working together more effective.*

Working as a team member is an important skill in today's workplace. Many industries assign teams of employees to work on projects. Each employee brings a different skill to the team. Teamwork is also important in other situations. For example, in organizing a school fund-raiser, each person on the committee may have a specific role.

Working in a group can also make learning more productive and enjoyable. In order to work together, you must be able to communicate clearly with your group members.

CONSIDER

?

1. **What does it mean to communicate?**
2. **How can everyone in a group be encouraged to participate?**
3. **When you're working in a group, when should you ask the teacher for help?**

In the following Explore, you will have a chance to work with your classmates. Be sure to pay attention to how well your group is working as a team!

EXPLORE: FIGURE IT OUT!

Figures such as the ones shown here are an important part of a geometry textbook.

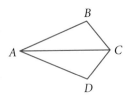

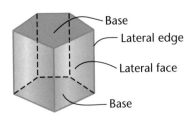

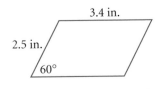

1. Work in a group to estimate how many such figures are contained in this book.
2. Does everyone in your group agree with the final estimate? Why or why not?
3. Compare your group's estimate with those of other groups. Were your estimates very different? Do you want to revise your estimate?

Working in a group can be an exciting way to learn mathematics. Throughout this course, you will have many opportunities to team up with your classmates.

REFLECT

1. Develop a list of at least five rules for successful cooperative groups. These rules should address any problems you may have had working in a group in the preceding Explore.
2. Describe some ways in which working in a group may be helpful to you throughout this course.

Exercises

1. Describe a situation in which you were part of a team (for example, a club or a sports team). What were the advantages and disadvantages of being part of this group? Were you able to do things with the group that you couldn't have done individually?

The following figures all occur elsewhere in this textbook. Using what you already know about geometry, describe each figure as best you can. (You will learn more about each figure later.)

2.

3.

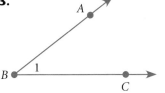

4.

5.

6.

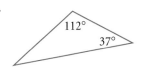

7.

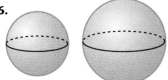

← CONNECT → *You have solved many mathematical problems before taking this class, and you have probably already used some type of problem-solving guidelines and strategies. All of these strategies and techniques can be used in this class.*

Problem solving does not mean just finding the answer to a problem in a math book! All through our lives we are presented with new and challenging problems. Learning to think critically and creatively gives us the ability (mathematical and otherwise) to solve the problems we encounter.

CONSIDER

1. What are some different strategies you have used to solve problems?
2. If you do not immediately understand a problem, what are some things you can do to help get started?

Whenever the solution to a problem is not immediately apparent, it may be helpful to follow some guidelines and questions for problem solving, such as the ones listed below.

PROBLEM-SOLVING GUIDELINES

Understand the Problem	**Develop a Plan**
What is the situation all about?	Have you ever worked a
What are you trying to find out?	similar problem before?
What are the key data/conditions?	Will you estimate or calculate?
What are the assumptions?	What strategies can you use?
Implement the Plan	**Look Back**
What is the solution?	Could you work the problem
Did you interpret correctly?	another way?
Did you calculate correctly?	Is there another solution?
Did you answer the question?	Is the answer reasonable?

1. How many squares are contained in the figure at the right? (Be sure to consider squares of various sizes.)

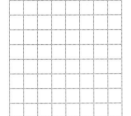

> **Problem-Solving Tip**
>
> Make a table.

2. Describe the process you used to solve this problem. Is there anything you might have done differently? If so, what?

Have you ever had the feeling of a light bulb going on when you made a new discovery or solved a challenging problem? This book is dedicated to that rewarding "aha!" feeling. We hope many light bulbs will go on as you use this textbook.

REFLECT

1. You may have used the strategy of making a table in the preceding Explore. List some other common strategies for solving problems.

2. Can you think of anything to add to the Problem-Solving Guidelines on the preceding page? If so, describe a situation in which your suggestion might be useful.

Exercises

1. a. Farmer McDonald raises cows and ducks. He is standing in his field and sees 9 heads and 26 feet. How many ducks and how many cows does Farmer McDonald have?

b. Describe the process you used to solve this problem.

2. The figure at the right shows the water level of a bathtub over time. Write a short paragraph to describe what might have occurred.

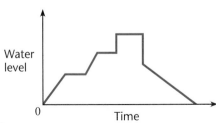

3. What is the maximum number of pieces into which a circular pizza can be cut with 4 straight cuts? (The pieces cannot be moved or stacked after cuts are made.)

← C O N N E C T → *You have seen how to use problem-solving guidelines to help you solve problems, and you have practiced working in a group. Now you will use these skills as we look at other important techniques.*

As you use this book, you will have many opportunities to work in groups (in Explore activities) and many opportunities to practice what you have learned (in Try It activities). You will also look at how the topics you learn are connected to each other, and you will see how mathematics is connected to other things.

Another important component of this book is a feature called What Do YOU Think? There is often more than one correct way to approach a problem. The students you have been introduced to on page *i* will be sharing their thinking throughout this book. You may find that you agree with their thinking, or you may have your own ideas.

WHAT DO **YOU** THINK?

Describe the connection between the equation on the left and the figure on the right.

$y = 3x + 2$

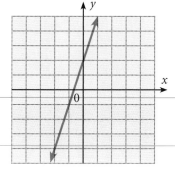

Henry Thinks . . .

I can make a table of values for the equation $y = 3x + 2$. If I plot these points, they will lie on a straight line. The line is the one shown in the graph.

x	y
−1	−1
0	2
1	5

Heather Thinks . . .

The equation is in the form $y = mx + b$. The value of m is 3, and this is the slope of the graph of the equation. The value of b is 2, and this means that the y-intercept of the graph is 2. If I put those two things together, I get the line in the figure.

CONSIDER

1. Do you agree with Heather and Henry's thinking? Can you think of another way to describe the connection between the equation and the graph on the preceding page?

You will often be asked to explain your thinking. As you study geometry, you may find that *how* you communicate your thoughts is as important as getting the "right answer."

REFLECT

1. Describe two different methods for solving a problem that you studied in a previous course. Discuss the advantages or disadvantages of each method.

2. Why do you think it is important to understand the connections between mathematics and other disciplines?

3. Why do you think it is important to understand the connections between different subjects within mathematics?

Exercises

1. Describe the connection between the figure below left and the figure on the right.

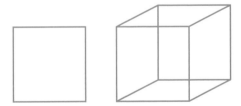

2. Write a short paragraph describing the optical illusion shown at the right.

3. There is an important connection between geometry and language. Make a chart that illustrates basic geometric figures. For each figure, include a sketch as well as a brief written description of the figure. If you know the names of the figures, be sure to include them.

Chapter 1

Project A

May I Have a Moment of Your Time?

Did you ever take part in a survey? Who decides what questions will be asked?

Project B

How Do You Get There From Here?

How are city maps made? How are they different from other maps?

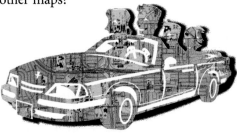

Project C

Let Nature Unfold

How does nature mirror itself? Why don't you have two left feet?